I0626903

The First Step

Why Obedience Matters

Melody Lavin

The First Step: Why Obedience Matters
Copyright © 2024 Melody Lavin

All rights reserved. This book or any portion thereof may not be reproduced or used in any manner whatsoever without the express written permission of the publisher except for the use of brief quotations in a book review.

Scripture quotations marked NASB are taken from the New American Standard Bible®. Copyright © 1960, 1971, 1977, 1995 by The Lockman Foundation. Used by permission. All rights reserved.

Scripture quotations marked ESV are taken from the The Holy Bible, English Standard Version®. Copyright © 2001 by Crossway, a publishing ministry of Good News Publishers. Used by permission. All rights reserved.

Scripture quotations marked NLT are taken from the Holy Bible, New Living Translation. Copyright © 1996, 2004, 2015 by Tyndale House Foundation. Used by permission of Tyndale House Publishers, Carol Stream, Illinois 60188. All rights reserved.

Scripture quotations marked MSG are taken from The Message. Copyright © 1993, 2002, 2018 by Eugene H. Peterson. Used by permission of NavPress. All rights reserved. Represented by Tyndale House Publishers.

Paperback ISBN: 979-8-9906565-1-2
eBook ISBN: 979-8-9906565-0-5
Library of Congress Control Number: 2025901632

Printed in the United States of America

Published in the United States of America
by Guided Path Publishing, Tennessee

GUIDED PATH
PUBLISHING

Preface

I'm not a novelist, but I knew that to make this book relatable, I should introduce you to some real people. They lived many years ago, and to introduce their situations to you, I took some liberty when writing their thoughts and conversations. I directly quoted scripture when referencing God's statements to them since that's appropriate. I imagine that Samuel, Saul, and David had thoughts and feelings like we have even though their time and location differ from ours. They faced things that we face. We can learn from them.

Table of Contents

The First Step

He realized that it wasn't going to be easy to do what everyone had told him they wanted. Placing one foot on the hard-packed earth, he started his journey toward the destiny they had chosen. His heart ached. He knew what their decision would cost them.

Samuel didn't want to anoint a king for Israel, but the people had demanded a king so they could be like other nations. That demand took Israel away from God as their king and propelled them toward a flawed man's rule.

In the stories of Samuel, Saul, and David we see the joy of obedience and the devastating results of disobedience toward God. Can we learn from both their mistakes and their commitments to a relationship with God? If we can learn, then we can develop into who

God created us to be—people who have a meaningful relationship with Him and a passion to use the gifts He gave us to help others.

Relationship Changes Everything

Samuel rubbed his eyes sleepily. Why was Eli calling him? It was the middle of the night. Pushing his tired little body to his feet, he padded to Eli's apartment. "Here I am. You called me."

"What?" mumbled Eli. "Oh no. I didn't call you. Go back to sleep boy."

Samuel quietly walked back to his sleeping pallet in the room where the Ark of the Covenant stood. He never tired of remembering God's deliverance of His people from Egypt. Samuel lay down again and slowly began to drift off to sleep.

"Samuel!"

Samuel awoke from his dozing and again walked to Eli. "Here I am. You called me."

"No, I didn't call you. Now go back to sleep." Eli rolled over and tried to get comfortable after the interruption.

With a sigh, Samuel walked back to his pallet and lay down again.

"Samuel!"

This time, Samuel jumped up and walked quickly to Eli. "Here I am. You called me."

"No, I didn't call you. But wait, it's God who is calling you. Go lie down again, and if He calls again, say, 'Speak, LORD, for your servant hears.'"

Samuel agreed and walked back to his pallet. Lying down, he waited for God to call again.

"Samuel! Samuel!"

Samuel sat up and said, "Speak for your servant hears." God began to speak. It was the beginning of many personal conversations they would have. It was the beginning of a relationship.

■ ■

Samuel may have been young, but God wanted to talk to him, to get to know him, and to be known. God wants to have a relationship with you and me as well. His desire for relationship is at the foundation of

His interactions with people. From the beginning of recorded biblical history, we see God talking and engaging with people. Genesis 3:8 says that God came to the garden of Eden in the cool of the day to see Adam and Eve. It was as if He was saying by His actions, "I want to know you, to be with you, to talk with you, to have a long-term relationship with you."

Throughout the Bible we see God continually interacting with people like Abraham and Sarah, Enoch, Noah, Moses, Miriam, Deborah and so many more on into the New Testament. The Bible records actual accounts of people's lives that were profoundly changed by knowing God.

A relationship with God is based on His love for us and our response to His love. Because of His love for us, He sent His Son to create the way for our salvation from sin. Someone told us about this; that God wasn't distant, and He could be known. Our response to Him in accepting His love and His Son started the relationship. Acceptance changed everything.

God wants to be known. He communicates, reveals His unique plan for your life, and provides direction for you. He speaks to you through the Bible and by the prompting of His Spirit. You can trust that He wants you to have what's best for you. That trust is based on His character. You can evaluate His character by reading the Bible and seeing how He interacted with people in the past. He has clearly stated His thoughts and demonstrated consistent actions. God can be known.

Your relationship with God is not static; it's dynamic. It continues to grow and develop as you actively pursue knowing Him. God is not one-dimensional. His character is multi-faceted. Getting to know Him is a lifelong experience. The more you pursue knowing Him, the more you see that He isn't distant; He's knowable, relatable, and personable.

What does a relationship with God look like?

I'd like to answer that question with scriptures. In John 15, Jesus talked about the concept of *abiding in Him*, being a part of Him. We're not really able to understand this from an example in our current culture because it's a spiritual concept. Jesus was talking about a new life in the family of God from a spiritual perspective. The words in John 15:4–5 were spoken to people who believed in Him—who had committed their lives to follow Him as disciples.

> "Abide in Me, and I in you. As the branch cannot bear fruit of itself unless it abides in the vine, so neither can you unless you abide in Me. I am the vine, you are the branches; he who abides in Me and I in him, he bears much fruit, for apart from Me you can do nothing." NASB

Here is a perspective about *abiding* that has helped me. The word *abide* contains the meaning of living somewhere, remaining and staying there. In other words, once you've begun the relationship, you stay in it and continue to develop it.

Our relationship with God puts us in a spiritual position in God's family that many people don't understand. Paul the apostle prayed that we would comprehend what God had done for us to make the relationship possible. Paul prayed that we would know the greatness of God's power seen as He raised Jesus from the dead and "seated Him at His right hand in the heavenly places, far above all rule and authority and power and dominion, and every name that is named, not only in this age but also in the one to come. And He put all things in subjection under His feet, and gave Him as head over all things to the church, which is His body...." Ephesians 1:20-23 NASB

In Ephesians 2, Paul described our previous spiritual condition as being dead in our sin. Then he explained, "But God, being rich in mercy, because of His great love with which He loved us, even when we were dead in our transgressions, made us alive together with Christ (by grace you have been saved), and raised us up with Him, and seated us with Him in the heavenly places in Christ Jesus." Ephesians 2:4–6 NASB

Your spiritual position in the family of God is *in Christ*, and He is seated at the right hand of God the

Father. So you are *in Christ at the right hand of God the Father.* Jesus prayed that we would be one with Him and the Father. He said, "that they may all be one; even as You, Father, are in Me and I in You, that they also may be in Us, so that the world may believe that You sent Me. The glory which You have given Me I have given to them, that they may be one, just as We are one; I in them and You in Me." John 17:21–23 NASB

If your position is *in Christ,* who is seated at the Father's right hand, then prayer is exceptionally easy. You can think of yourself spiritually turning to your left and thanking the Father God for what He has provided for you through Jesus Christ. Your prayers that remind God of what He has said in the Bible please Him, and your words of thanks spoken from your faith in Him release the blessings that He has already provided for you. Paul also wrote, "Blessed be the God and Father of our Lord Jesus Christ, who has blessed us with every spiritual blessing in the heavenly places in Christ." Ephesians 1:3 NASB

Abiding in that relationship produces an experiential knowledge of God. You abide in Him and His words from the Bible abide in you. His Word is His stated will. When you allow God's Word (the Bible) to live in you to the same extent that you live in Him, the results are profound. You will have an ongoing experiential revelation of Him, you will see how Jesus did the works of the Father, and you will become full of God's Word—His will. Jesus said, "If you abide in Me, and My words abide in you, ask whatever you wish, and it will be done for you." John 15:7 NASB

> "This is the confidence which we have before Him, that, if we ask anything according to His will, He hears us. And if we know that He hears us in whatever we ask, we know that we have the requests which we have asked from Him." 1 John 5:14–15 NASB

This also emphasizes the power of Jesus' words in Mark 11:23–24 where He spoke both about the power of command from His position far above everything and the power of prayer, knowing that everything that we need has been provided through Him and His sacrifice. "Truly, I say to you, whoever says to this mountain, 'Be taken up and thrown into the sea,' and does not doubt in his heart, but believes that what he says will come to pass, it will be done for him. Therefore I tell you, whatever you ask in prayer, believe that you have received it, and it will be yours." ESV

Those are authoritative statements. Your faith in God—that He is who He says He is and that He will do what He says that He will do—is released 1) when you command a challenge to move, and 2) when you pray, believing that you have received what you have asked. Faith is the currency of Heaven. Your faith enforces your words and *receives* the blessing that has already been provided through Jesus.

Your position in Jesus Christ is not one where you come and go. You remain in Him. Your spiritual position is in the throne room. A continual awareness of the throne room produces three things:

1. Worship that is continual and is focused on God— to Him and about Him—as we see in Revelation chapter 4.

2. Prayer that is faith-based and powerful, without begging and tears.

3. Obedience as the result of your ongoing love-based relationship with God.

It will not be difficult to obey God when you are talking and listening to Him, when you live in a continual awareness of His will through His Word, and when you are participating in continual worship of Him.

Remember your position and look to your left.

CHAPTER TWO

Relationship Must Have Depth

That day was like any other day, except it wasn't. The elders of Israel stood in the warm sun surrounded by the natural perfume of grass and earth. They should have been relaxed by the drone of lazy insects and the low murmur of people nearby, but their gazes were hard and their shoulders were tense when their leader spoke.

"Samuel, your sons sin. They aren't following the commandments of God. They've disqualified themselves from judging the people. We've decided that we don't want you to replace them with other judges. Give us a king. Appoint a king to judge us like all the other nations have."

No, it's not right, thought Samuel. *I won't do it. I have to pray.*

God responded as Samuel prayed. "Listen to the voice of the people in regard to all that they say to you, for they have not rejected you, but they have rejected Me from being king over them. Like all the deeds which they have done since the day that I brought them up from Egypt even to this day—in that they have forsaken Me and served other gods—so they are doing to you also. Now then, listen to their voice; however, you shall solemnly warn them and tell them of the procedure of the king who will reign over them,"[1]

And so began the disobedience of a nation that rejected their Creator and true King.

What do you do when the people around you choose a course that defies God? You continue to obey Him. Samuel learned to follow God's voice when he was young. He never stopped listening. He said what God told him to say. He did what God told him to do. He had a deep relationship with God. When the elders pushed Samuel to appoint a king and he knew that it was wrong, he talked to God. Samuel prayed and he listened when God spoke. Then he obeyed. His obedience was a result of his commitment to his deep relationship with God.

Obedience is a result of a *committed relationship*. Jesus' relationship with His Father demonstrates that.

He said in John 5:30, "I can do nothing on My own initiative. As I hear, I judge; and My judgement is just,
because I do not seek My own will, but the will of Him
who sent Me." NASB He said in John 4:34, "My food is to
do the will of Him who sent Me and to accomplish His
work." NASB

Jesus was sustained, not drained, as He did the
Father God's will. When we read the book of John chap-
ters 14–17, we see Jesus' unified relationship with the
Father. Because He is *one* with the Father, He does what
the Father directs and says what the Father wants to
be said. In John 14:8, Philip said, "'Lord, show us the
Father, and it is enough for us.' Jesus said to him, 'Have
I been so long with you, and yet you have not come to
know Me, Philip? He who has seen Me has seen the
Father; how can you say, "Show us the Father"? Do you
not believe that I am in the Father, and the Father is in
Me? The words that I say to you I do not speak on My
own initiative, but the Father abiding in Me does His
works.'" NASB How can Jesus say that? Because He and
His Father were *one*—completely united.

We have that kind of unity with the Father God
through Jesus Christ. We saw that in chapter one when
we looked at John 15:4–5. The illustration in John 15 of
a vine and branches lends itself to the use of the word
fruit as describing what the branch produces—the
results of deriving connection and nourishment from a
particular type of plant. The key in John 15:1–17 is the

description of the source. Jesus is the source. In John chapter 14, He clearly stated that He said and did what His Father directed because He and His Father were completely united. In the same way, we are united in Jesus. Because of that, when you abide in Him, you will act like Him and produce what He produced.

The fruit is seen in Jesus' life—in His words and actions. Your commission to reproduce His words and actions is seen in John 14:12, "whoever believes in me will also do the works that I do; and greater works than these will he do, because I am going to the Father." ESV We also see that commission in Jesus' words in Matthew 28:18–20, "All authority in heaven and on earth has been given to me. Go therefore and make disciples of all nations, baptizing them in the name of the Father and of the Son and of the Holy Spirit, teaching them to observe all that I have commanded you." ESV

Why should we be obedient to follow Jesus' instructions? Jesus said, "My Father is glorified by this, that you bear much fruit, and so prove to be My disciples" and, "You did not choose Me but I chose you, and appointed you that you would go and bear fruit, and that your fruit would remain, so that whatever you ask of the Father in My name He may give to you." John 15:8, 16 NASB Do you see the interconnection of your life in Him and the results of that life? Obedience facilitates the production of fruit in your life.

Your response to God's direction is to obey what He communicates and reveals. Your obedience to God is not blind obedience. You will know who you are following. In your relationship with Him, you recognize and accept that He sees things that you cannot see. If God asks you to do something out of the ordinary, He will have uniquely designed you to handle it, and He will have provided the desire to do it.

The motive for obedience is love for God. We love and trust God; therefore, obeying Him makes sense. Obedience to what God encourages and instructs you to do should not be the result of a sense of obligation; it should be the result of your love for Him in your profound relationship together. Obedience is not defined by actions that are the result of fear or forced submission. Obedience is defined by an attitude of trust in God, respect for His wisdom, love for Him, and actions that honor His direction. Jesus said that the motive for obedience is love for God. "But I do as the Father has commanded me, so that the world may know that I love the Father." John 14:31 ESV Another translation states it this way, "But so the world might know how thoroughly I love the Father, I am carrying out my Father's instructions right down to the last detail." MSG

Obedience is your part of the relationship. When you do your part, God responds with His part. We stop Him from doing His part of the relationship with us when we don't do our part. Many times we've said, "No" to the prompting of God to do something. Maybe what He's prompted would be uncomfortable or would require our time or resources. But when we say "No," we stop ourselves from the opportunity to be positioned in His plan. God knows more than we know. He's eternal and can see past, present, and future. Do you want what He has prepared for you in your future? If so, then follow His direction now.

The depth of your relationship with God will be reflected in your obedience to Him.

CHAPTER THREE

Humility Is the Attitude of Obedience

Samuel sat on a cool block of stone with his eyes closed. He rested his head back against the tree that covered him in shade. A whisper of air danced across his cheek, and he sighed. It felt like a weight—this responsibility to speak for God to His people. They didn't understand the relationship. They only knew that God spoke to him.

Today he was at home, in Ramah, waiting on God—making the time to reverence Him and to listen. What did God want to say, and when did He want to say it? If only God's people could understand that He wanted to talk to them, to interact with them, and to be their God and king.

Samuel sighed again. It was time to do the annual travel circuit to Bethel, Gilgal, and Mizpah. It was time to judge the people's concerns and issues. "God gives strength," he said. "God gives His wisdom. I will not do this in my strength or wisdom."

■ ■

Samuel was humble before God. His humility was seen in his service to God, in his steadfastness to God's commandment, and in his commitment to serve God's people. He was submitted to God's direction.

We also see submission to God's will in Jesus' life. To fully understand how Jesus could submit His will to obey the Father when He was here on earth and was tempted like we are (Hebrews 4:14-15), we need to study the concept of humility. Paul wrote about this in Philippians 2:5-8.

> "Have this attitude in yourselves which was also in Christ Jesus, who, although He existed in the form of God, did not regard equality with God a thing to be grasped, but emptied Himself, taking the form of a bond-servant, and being made in the likeness of men. Being found in appearance as a man, He humbled Himself by becoming obedient to the point of death, even death on a cross." NASB

Jesus submitted Himself to the Father's will, positioning Himself as a servant who understood God's vision for our rescue from sin. Jesus didn't consider obedience too great a price to pay. His purpose was clear, and He emptied Himself of the glory that He had with the Father. He said in John 17:4-5, "I glorified You on the earth, having accomplished the work which You have given Me to do. Now, Father, glorify Me together with Yourself, with the glory which I had with You before the world was." NASB

Jesus humbled Himself. The Father didn't humble Jesus; Jesus humbled Himself.

What is so important about humility? Paul wrote, "have this attitude in yourselves which was also in Christ Jesus...." Philippians 2:5 NASB *Humility inspires submission.* In Philippians 2:8 we see Jesus' action of submitting Himself to the point of ultimate obedience to the Father's plan—death on the cross. In Jesus' example, we see that *humility is an attitude that inspires action.*

Paul's words prior to his description of Jesus reveal a practical application of humility. He wrote, "Do nothing from selfishness or empty conceit, but with humility of mind regard one another as more important than yourselves; do not merely look out for your own personal interests, but also for the interests of others." Philippians 2:3-4 NASB

Attitudes of self-promotion, self-focus, selfishness, arrogance, pride, and stubbornness are resistant to obedience to God.

True submission of yourself to God requires the emptying of your desires and wants. Instead, recognition and corresponding actions toward Jesus' lordship are required. The concept of Jesus' lordship is something that makes some people uncomfortable because they don't want to relinquish control of their lives. Regardless, it's necessary. Paul revealed the way to true salvation: "if you confess with your mouth Jesus as Lord, and believe in your heart that God raised Him from the dead, you will be saved; for with the heart a person believes, resulting in righteousness, and with the mouth he confesses, resulting in salvation." Romans 10:9-10 NASB Paul also wrote about his own salvation saying, "I have been crucified with Christ; and it is no longer I who live, but Christ lives in me; and the life which I now live in the flesh I live by faith in the Son of God, who loved me and gave Himself up for me." Galatians 2:20 NASB

When you let go of your desires as you submit to Jesus as Lord you will be truly abiding in Him, representing Him as He directs you. You will produce the fruit of actions that please the Father just as Jesus did (John 4:34; 5:30; 14:12; 15:8.) You will be empowered and positioned to be who and what you were created to be.

"So then, my beloved, just as you have
always obeyed, not as in my presence only,
but now much more in my absence, work

out your salvation with fear and trembling;
for it is God who is at work in you, both to
will and to work for His good pleasure. Do
all things without grumbling or disputing."
Philippians 2:12-14 NASB

Humility toward God involves seeking Him for His
direction and guidance, listening for that guidance
given by His Spirit, and obeying and acting on that guidance. True humility is seen in love, self-sacrifice, and
honoring what God wants you to do in serving others.

An attitude of humility is seen as we approach
leadership and ministry as *service* to others. That service given out of the source of love becomes a true joy to
us. You can serve others and not consider it a waste of
time if you do it as Jesus did—giving Himself for others.
Paul wrote, "Therefore be imitators of God, as beloved
children; and walk in love, just as Christ also loved you
and gave Himself up for us, an offering and a sacrifice
to God as a fragrant aroma." Ephesians 5:1-2 NASB

In the struggle to be heard, arrogant people will take
advantage of opportunities and will promote a personal
agenda. I have seen in my many years of ministry that it
is possible for a minister or leader to forget how important it is to help people resolve conflict, to overcome an
offense, or to commit themselves to change and learn.
It's possible to be so caught up in enforcing that you are
a pastor or leader that you forget what a pastor *is* and
does. Being so caught up in the title, the structure, the

desire for honor that you forget that Jesus set a sacrificial example for all of us as He washed the disciples' feet, agonized in prayer at Gethsemane, and gave everything on the cross.

Nothing is of more value than service to others as God directs. No pontificating, building a massive church building, establishing a huge social media presence, or expanding a personal sphere of influence compares to the honor it is to serve others as Jesus served. Until we recognize what true service is, we will not humble ourselves, obey God, and put others first. God honors humility.

> "God is opposed to the proud, but gives grace to the humble. Submit therefore to God. Resist the devil and he will flee from you. Draw near to God and He will draw near to you. Cleanse your hands, you sinners; and purify your hearts, you double-minded. Be miserable and mourn and weep; let your laughter be turned into mourning and your joy to gloom. Humble yourselves in the presence of the Lord, and He will exalt you." James 4:6-10 NASB

People do not honor humility because it doesn't look like their version of success. True success is achieved through obedience. It is achieved through a determination to leave behind whatever would promote you and instead promote God and His ideas—His Word. Success is dependent upon your attitude of humility and actions of obedience. There is no success in the Kingdom of God outside of that.

Jesus said, "Truly I say to you, unless you are converted and become like children, you will not enter the kingdom of heaven. Whoever then humbles himself as this child, he is the greatest in the kingdom of heaven. And whoever receives one such child in My name receives Me." Matthew 18:3-5 NASB He also said, "But the greatest among you shall be your servant. Whoever exalts himself shall be humbled; and whoever humbles himself shall be exalted." Matthew 23:11-12 NASB

When you have an attitude of humility, preeminence means nothing to you. You have a higher goal: exalting Jesus, pointing toward Him in all that you do and say.

It's also important to note than an attitude of humility is not an attitude of worthlessness. Paul wrote the following truths about the born-again believer.

"But God, being rich in mercy, because of His great love with which He loved us, even when we were dead in our transgressions, made us alive together with Christ (by grace you have been saved), and raised us up with Him, and seated us with Him in the heavenly places in Christ Jesus." Ephesians 2:4-6 NASB

"For if, because of one man's trespass, death reigned through that one man, much more will those who receive the abundance of

grace and the free gift of righteousness reign
in life through the one man Jesus Christ."
Romans 5:17 ESV

An attitude of humility comes from seeing yourself
in Jesus. Instead of focusing on developing self-esteem,
develop a knowledge and awareness of *who you are in
Jesus Christ.*

So what actions does humility inspire in our lives?
Here are Peter's instructions that clearly show us how
we can live a life of humility.

"Likewise, you who are younger, be subject to
the elders. Clothe yourselves, all of you, with
humility toward one another, for 'God opposes
the proud but gives grace to the humble.'
Humble yourselves, therefore, under the
mighty hand of God so that at the proper time
he may exalt you, casting all your anxieties on
him, because he cares for you." 1 Peter 5:5-7 ESV

"As each has received a gift, use it to serve
one another, as good stewards of God's varied
grace." 1 Peter 4:10 ESV.

In the same way, Paul encouraged us with practical
application in Colossians 3:12 and Ephesians chapter
four where he covered these concepts: demonstrating
humility, gentleness and patience toward others from
a heart filled with God's love; being eager to maintain
the unity of the Spirit; not being like children who are

tossed about by every teaching and scheme; speaking the truth in love; growing up in all areas, working properly; doing our part; avoiding the mental futility of the world; being renewed in the spirit of our mind; living a life that reflects the newness that was created in our spirit in true righteousness and holiness; speaking the truth; not allowing anger to remain or to control us; putting aside all intense anger; working and sharing—not stealing; only speaking good with grace; avoiding bitterness and slander; being kind; forgiving; walking in love as a child of God who represents his or her Father.

Additionally, humility is a recognition that we don't know everything. The older we become, the more we see how much we don't know. It isn't that the knowledge isn't available; it's that we haven't met the person who has the piece of knowledge that we need. Paul wrote in Ephesians chapter four that every part of the Body of Christ has something to give. Every person in the Body of Christ has a gift that is supposed to connect to other parts of the Body of Christ. Not everyone is inspired by God to write books, do podcasts, put something on social media, or be on television, but that doesn't mean that they don't have something that you need. To make that connection, you can pray that God would lead you to divine appointments. When you are in those divine appointments, keep your opinions to yourself and receive the nugget of knowledge or the gift, skill, or talent that the person has that you need in order to grow.

When you are truly humble, you will learn when to talk and when to receive. You'll listen and learn, understanding that learning from and with others is a life-long adventure.

There is no true obedience without humility.

CHAPTER FOUR

Stewardship is Obedience in Action

The sun was hot on David's head. He loved its warmth and he lifted his face toward the brightness. It soothed him and rippled down his spine. "How I love your ways my God," he said. "In Your presence is fullness of joy. You have delivered me from the lion and the bear. You are my strength." David looked intently at the sheep he was guarding, and then focused his eyes on the distance, scanning the area for threats.

David was a steward. He understood his father's authority to direct his employment, and he understood his personal responsibility to care for what had been entrusted to him. The safety and care that David provided for the sheep created an environment where they could multiply. Their numbers could increase because of David's obedience to his father's instructions.

In the same way, God entrusts certain things to our care. He expects us to manage or steward them. Here is a general understanding of the words *to steward something* that are and have been used: manage, oversee, administer something as a representative or agent; protect something for which you have been given responsibility.

In Matthew 25:14-29, Jesus told the parable of the talents. The talents were monetary amounts that a person entrusted to his employees.

"For it will be like a man going on a journey, who called his servants and entrusted to them his property. To one he gave five talents, to another two, to another one, to each according to his ability. Then he went away. He who had received the five talents went at once and traded with them, and he made five talents more. So also he who had the two talents made two talents more. But he who had received the one talent went and dug in the ground and hid his master's money. Now after a long time the master of those servants came and settled accounts with them. And he who had received the five talents came forward, bringing five talents more, saying, 'Master, you delivered to me five talents; here I have made five talents more.' His master said to him, 'Well done, good and faithful servant. You have been faithful over a little; I will set you over much. Enter into the joy of your master.' And he also who had the two talents came forward, saying, 'Master, you delivered to me two talents; here I have made two talents more.' His master said to him, 'Well done, good and faithful servant. You have been faithful over a little; I will set you over much. Enter into the joy of your master.' He also who had received the one talent came forward, saying, 'Master, I knew you to be a hard man, reaping where you did not sow, and gathering where you scattered no seed, so I was afraid, and I went and hid your talent in the ground. Here you have what is yours.' But his master answered him, 'You wicked and slothful servant! You knew that I reap where I have not sown and gather where I scattered no seed? Then you ought to have invested my money with the bankers, and at my coming I should have received what was my own with interest. So take the talent from him and give it to him who has the ten talents. For to everyone who has will more be given, and he will have an abundance. But from the one who has not, even what he has will be taken away." ESV

The employer looked at each employee's ability and gave them the amount that he thought corresponded with their skills. It's important to note that in this parable, one talent was a monetary unit that may have been worth fifteen or twenty years of wages for a laborer. Each employee was faced with the opportunity to run away with the money. Within the parable we see that the employer's end goals were to 1) test the employees' faithfulness and their willingness to steward the amount, and 2) to create and receive an increase of what had been entrusted to their care.

Two of the employees in the parable displayed faithfulness and skill by immediately investing in business; they traded with those talents. Their obedience to use their skill caused multiplication. They didn't just produce one more talent; they doubled what they had been given. They knew their employer; they knew his character and expectations.

In the same way, God has given each of us the opportunity to steward resources. The way in which we manage the resources that God has given to us reflects the respect and honor that we have for Him.

Stewardship is a missing component in many people's lives. They have been entrusted with hours of time, money, health, life, family relationships, and friends. Yet it seems to be not enough because their focus is on the *getting, the having, the want* instead of on the stewardship, the obedience, and getting God's plan for the proper use of those resources. They have not focused on *why* they were blessed with them and *how* each resource fits into God's plan for their lives.

To squander any of those resources is to disobey God's plan and direction. *To squander* is to determine within oneself how something should be used. Failure occurs.

Resources that have been provided for one thing should never be used for another thing. Those resources were not designed for the other thing; they were not provided by God for the other thing. We need to ask God to tell us how we can most effectively use the resources that He has provided.

In Luke 4:1-4, we see that Jesus had the resource of power. In verse 3, the devil told him to turn a stone to bread. The resource of power was not to be used for that purpose. Why did Jesus have power? He explains it later in that narrative in Luke 4:18-19 where He says, "The Spirit of the LORD is upon Me, because He anointed Me to preach the gospel to the poor. He has sent Me to proclaim release to the captives, and recovery of sight to the blind, to set free those who are oppressed, to proclaim the favorable year of the LORD." NASB The power for freedom is not to be squandered on making bread from a stone. It is to be used to glorify God, to set people free, and to do His work in His time and place. You need to know the purpose for which the resource is to be used.

The principle of obedience in stewardship includes more than tithing. It includes stewarding all resources.

The most valuable resource we have is *time*. With time we make money, we raise our children, we create and maintain relationships, and share the Gospel. We have a certain number of hours in our lives. We may not know how many hours we have, but we do have the responsibility to use them as good stewards.

> *If you cannot manage your time, why would you expect that God would entrust other resources to your care?*

The way in which we manage resources also shows whether we respect and honor God and the people that we work with. For example, we disrespect others by refusing to be good stewards of our time. When we commit to be somewhere at a specific time, then stewardship encompasses the budgeting of time—taking into consideration all of the factors that would cause us to be late, and compensating for them. In the case of a team meeting or a church service, lack of effective personal time management that creates a delay in our arrival at the scheduled meeting is a sign of disrespect toward the other team members. Being chronically late is a way in which we show that the other team members are not as important as we perceive ourselves to be, and the meeting and our service to God are not as important as other things in our lives. It shows that we are not fully committed to those people or to God.

■ ■

Humming to himself, David glanced to his left and saw someone running toward him across the grazing field.

"David," the young man panted as he came closer, "You're wanted at the house immediately."

"Why? Is something wrong?"

"No, but the prophet Samuel has come to offer a sacrifice, and your presence is required."

"All right. Stay with the sheep. I'll go quickly."

Samuel glanced up as Jesse said, "There he is. This is my youngest son, David." As Samuel looked at David, the Lord said, "Arise, anoint him; for this is he."[1] Samuel remembered God's words at Gilgal when he corrected Saul, "The LORD has sought out for himself a man after his own heart, and the LORD has appointed him as ruler over his people."[2] *This one has the Lord's heart,* Samuel thought. In front of David's incredulous brothers, Samuel poured oil on David, anointing him as God's chosen king. At that moment, the Spirit of God came upon David and remained, but the kingdom of Israel was not yet David's to rule. So David took his harp and went back to watching the sheep, protecting what had been entrusted to his care, learning the lessons he would need for the future.

David understood the value of instruction and the importance of timing. He recognized that what God had called him to do had a specific timing attached to it. If David had insisted on following God's call on his life with his own interpretation of how it should be done, then he would have missed God's direction. He stewarded the timing.

Timing is just as important as knowing what is the right thing to do.

Here are three steps that will help you to fulfill God's will for your life. They're simple, but they require your faith and your obedience. If you follow these steps, you will be stewarding God's instructions.

Step Number One: Get God's plan.

Ask God to show you or tell you what He would like you to do. This applies to the overall direction for your life, and it applies to individual situations and opportunities.

God created you in a specific way and gave you talents and abilities. It makes sense to ask Him these questions: "What do you want me to do with my life? What do you want me to do with this talent? What do you want me to do for a career? What do you want me to do today?"

Listen for God's direction. You can hear the Spirit of God as He speaks to your spirit. He lives in you (Galatians 4:6; 1 Corinthians 3:16). The Holy Spirit will reveal God's plan. Jesus said that the Holy Spirit is the Spirit of Truth and He will guide you into a knowledge of the truth.

> "I will ask the Father, and He will give you another Helper, that He may be with you forever; that is the Spirit of truth, whom the world cannot receive, because it does not see Him or know Him, but you know Him because He abides with you and will be in you." John 14:16-17 NASB

> "But when He, the Spirit of truth, comes, He will guide you into all the truth; for He will not speak on His own initiative, but whatever he hears, He will speak; and He will disclose to you what is to come." John 16:13 NASB

In Acts 8:29, the Holy Spirit spoke to Philip and told him what to do. "Then the Spirit said to Philip, 'Go up and join this chariot.'" NASB Philip's obedience to that instruction put him in a place where he was able to help the man in the chariot, teaching him the truth.

In Acts 10:19–20, the Holy Spirit spoke to Peter about what God wanted Peter to do. "While Peter was reflecting on the vision, the Spirit said to him, 'Behold, three men are looking for you. But get up, go downstairs and accompany them without misgivings, for I have sent them Myself.'" NASB Peter obeyed the instruction, and many people received salvation as a result.

Step Number Two: Get the details.

This is the step that most people miss. They hear from God and then immediately try to make it happen.

You may hear God's plan and say, "Now I know what to do. So, I want to start over here, and I'm going to do this now." If you are listening to God at that point, He will tell you, "That is the right thing to do, in the wrong place, at the wrong time."

Most of the time, we assume that we know what is best. In our arrogance, we miss God's plan because we neglect to get the details. Then we fail in our attempt, and we blame God.

In Genesis 15:1-4, God promised Abram that he would have a son. Abram heard God's plan. But Abram and Sarai decided to tell God how the promise should be fulfilled (Genesis 16:1-5). Sarai sent her servant, Hagar, to sleep with Abram. In Abram and Sarai's minds, they thought that since Abram was 86 and Sarai was around 76, God needed them to tell Him what was physically possible and what was impossible. Abram and Hagar created Ishmael. Ishmael was *not* the son that God had promised Abram. God's *plan* and its *details* were that the promised son would be the result of Abram and Sarai's union.

When you try to make the plan of God happen using your wisdom, you create an Ishmael. When you try to fulfill the will of God in your own strength, you miss the promise of God. You create something that will struggle with God's plan and will for your life.

The fulfillment of God's promise came to Abram and Sarai fourteen years after the promise had been given. "And the LORD did for Sarah as He had promised. So Sarah conceived and bore a son to Abraham in his old age, at the appointed time of which God had spoken to him." Genesis 21:1–2 NASB

Get the details of God's plan for your life. When the Holy Spirit tells you or shows you something, ask Him what you should do first. Ask for the *when*. Ask for the *where*. Ask for the *who*. You can ask questions like this: "Do you want me to do this now? In what way should I do this? Is this the right time? Are these the right people to work with? Where is the exact location?" Questions like that will open communication between God and you. You will be demonstrating your faith in God and your willingness to follow His direction as you pursue the details.

Step Number Three: Do the work step by step.

Once you have the details or a detail, and you know what, when, where, and with whom you are to do what God wants you to do, then *do it*. You may not always understand the step that He has asked you to do or *why* you should do it, but follow the instruction and *do it*. If God only gives you one step, then do that one. Then seek Him for the next step. Step by step, follow Him in faith. You know Him. You trust Him.

Instead of saying, "I'll make this work because this is what I want," let's change our attitude to: "What is best for me Lord? What should I do about it? When? In what way? With whom?" We will please God and we will be working and walking with Him hand-in-hand. It's vital to steward the instructions.

Obedience isn't an obligation; it's the result of trusting that God has a plan. It's your choice to follow the steps of that plan.

CHAPTER FIVE

Obedience Creates Opportunity

It really didn't make sense. There he was, sitting on a rock in the hot sun again watching sheep. *Well,* he thought, *I'll keep doing what I know to do, and when the king needs me again, he'll send someone for me. It's been a while since the king was troubled and I played my harp for him. He must be well; he's at the battlefront against the Philistines.* David shifted his position on the rock and looked over the flock.

That evening, Jesse said to David, "Son, I want you to take some supplies to your brothers at the battlefront. Check on your brothers and bring me news about them. You've been there before and you know the way, so take the supplies tomorrow, and then return. Don't delay in either direction."

"Yes Father, I'll be ready to go at first light."

Faint wisps of color teased the indigo of night from the sky when David closed the front door behind him. The supplies were waiting. *Here we go,* he thought, *another adventure. Every time Father sends me somewhere I see new things.*

As David reached the outskirts of the camp, the two armies were moving into fighting position and shouting their war cry. David quickly left his provisions with the supply officer and ran to his brother's position in the battle line. As he was talking to his brothers, a massive man stepped out of the Philistine camp and began to shout a challenge to the Israelite army to send someone to fight him. At the sight of Goliath the giant, the Israelite army began to run back toward the camp. They wailed, "There's no way anyone can fight this giant one-on-one and win. He's too big, too strong."

David stopped the men around him and asked, "What happens to the man who kills this Philistine and stops him from insulting Israel? What happens to the man who stops this shame? And who is this guy, this heathen Philistine, who's challenging God's army?"

One of the men said, "The king said that he would give the victor both wealth and his daughter as a bride, and the victor's father's household will be totally free from paying taxes."

Some of them heard what David was asking, and they told Saul, "There's a young man asking about the reward for killing Goliath."

"Bring him here," Saul said.

David stood before the king and said, "The people shouldn't fear this Philistine. I'll fight him."

Saul laughed, "You can't fight him; you're too young."

"Your servant may be young, but while I was watching my father's sheep, I fought and killed both lions and bears to protect the sheep. This Philistine is just like one of those attackers. The same God who delivered me from the lion and the bear will save me from this Philistine."

"Alright, go, and may God be with you. But here, first put on some of my armor."

"I'm sorry my king, but the armor doesn't fit. It's not mine, it's not made for me, and I haven't fought in it before."

David laid Saul's armor aside, picked up his stick, and chose five smooth stones from a nearby stream. He dropped the stones into his shepherd's bag and put his sling in his hand. *Let's do this,* he thought as he began to run toward Goliath.

Goliath looked down at David and began to curse. "Look kid, I'm going to feed you to the birds and the animals. You're nothing."

David said, "No, you're not. You come here with your sword, spear, and a javelin, but I come in the name of the LORD of hosts, the God of the army of Israel that you've been taunting. Your time is up. Today, right now, the LORD will give you to me, and I'll strike you down and cut off your head. Then I'll give the conquered, dead bodies of the Philistine army to the birds and the animals so everyone on earth will know that there is a God in Israel. And they'll all know that the LORD doesn't save by sword and spear because it's *His* battle, and *He* will give us the victory over you."

Grabbing a stone from his bag, David put it into his sling and slung it at Goliath. The stone hit the giant's forehead and sunk in. Goliath fell face first, shaking the ground when he hit. Dust choked the air as David ran forward. He pulled the giant's sword from its sheath and cut off Goliath's head. Seeing their victory, the Israelite army raced after the Philistines, killing them as they ran.

David's attitude and faith influenced his actions. He obeyed his father, his king, and his God. In every instance, David's obedience created opportunities to demonstrate further obedience and to ultimately act on God's behalf, helping His people.

David's actions also had positive results with regard to favor and prosperity. His actions started a chain of events in his life that brought him into the king's household where we read, "So David went out wherever Saul sent him, and prospered; and Saul set him over the men of war. And it was pleasing in the sight of all the people and also in the sight of Saul's servants." 1 Samuel 18:5 NASB In verse 14 we see that "David was prospering in all his ways for the LORD was with him." NASB

The wisdom that we see demonstrated by David was simple and pure.

Know God.

The time that David spent caring for his father's sheep gave him the opportunity to pray and worship God personally. He knew God's character, and he relied on and experienced God's strength within himself as he fought wild animals to protect the sheep.

Act on God's behalf.

When you know who God is in character and position, you won't tolerate disrespect toward Him. David not only defended Israel against Goliath and the Philistine army, he also defended and represented God's covenant with Israel.

Submit yourself to those in authority.

Humility enables you to submit yourself to authority. Submission to authority, including God's authority, will motivate you to obey. When you obey, you will find yourself in a position of opportunity in which you have new abundance, responsibilities, resources, and additional new opportunities to obey.

Honor what you are given to do and do it well.

When King Saul wanted David with him to minister in music, David did that. When King Saul sent David to fight, David did that. David didn't say no. He didn't procrastinate, which is disobedience. He didn't try to argue his case to do the instruction in a different way or at a different time. David received his commissions from the person in authority, and he did them with excellence.

To move forward, we must obey.

Your obedience creates the opportunity for the will of God to occur. Obedience puts you in the right place at the right time so you can receive an opportunity. It's like an American football game. The quarterback calls the play. You run the play as a receiver. The quarterback throws the ball to where you're supposed to be in the play. If you didn't follow the play and run it correctly, you won't be where the ball is after his throw. He will throw it to where you *should be*. You may have to scramble to get there but you need to execute the play so you can receive.

Your obedience unlocks opportunity.

Transition Requires Obedience

David was exhausted. So much running, trying to avoid being captured. Then there was the pressure of leading his men and ensuring the safety of their families. He sighed deeply in the cool darkness of the cave and leaned his head against a stone.

"Why God? Why does it have to be so hard?" he whispered. "Why can't the king be satisfied with his palace, his reputation, and the kingdom? Why does he hate me? I'm not attacking him. I haven't done anything wrong. And really, I never told him or anyone about that time when Samuel anointed me to be the next king. What's next? I know you've been showing me how to be a leader, but when will what I know about the future come to pass?"

A scrape and a muffled footstep broke David's words.

"David, there's something you need to see,"
one of his men whispered in David's ear.

"What is it? What do I need to see?" David
breathed.

"Shh, it's the king, and he's here in the cave
basically alone. You had us shelter farther back in
the cave, but I was on sentry duty when the king
came into the cave to relieve himself. What do you
want to do? We can attack, kill him, and seize the
kingdom. This must be God's doing; placing King
Saul into our hands."

They crept slowly through the back sections of the
cave, skirting around ancient shelves of rocks that
intruded into the passages. David felt the sweat trickle
down his back. He raised his hand, and they stopped.
Saul was up ahead, facing toward the front of the cav-
ern. Two guards were farther away. Their voices were a
low murmur.

"This is it," whispered David's man. "God has
delivered Saul into your hands. Kill him. Now."

"No. I won't raise my hand against someone
that God anointed. I will not try to make God's plan
happen in my timing, but I will give the king a
warning."

David crept closer to Saul. Breathing shallowly and
keeping his eyes slightly averted so Saul wouldn't feel

his stare, David saw that Saul's outer cloak had been tossed to the side. David crept forward until he reached the cloak. With a swift, clean slash of his knife, he cut off a piece of the cloak. Then he carefully moved backward until he had reached a large rock that would hide him from Saul's vision.

"What are you doing?" hissed the man. "We can take the king!"

"I won't do it," David whispered. "I shouldn't have even cut his cloak."

Saul stirred, stretched, and left the cave. He shouted, "Let's keep moving. We're going to find David and his men."

From the time that David was anointed to be the next king, until his ascension to the throne, he waited for years. In each opportunity for service, he worked, learned, grew, and positioned himself to be used by God. Transition occurred throughout his life, but the key to his success was that he did not try to make things happen. He did what he had been commissioned to do until it was time to do the next thing. In each season of life and service to God, David gave his complete focus to God's direction for that season.

David transitioned from shepherd to musician for the king, to a leader of armies. Later, he transitioned into kingship and was used in that role to display what open worship would be (1 Chronicles 16:1-7). David obeyed God's direction, honored God's presence, and led the people that God had entrusted to his care.

Transition occurs at all levels of our lives.

We tend to think that transition is only when big changes happen: a new job, a child going to college, a move to a new location. That's not true. Transition occurs in a thousand different small ways every day. We often call it growth. Sometimes it's physical growth upward or outward. At other times, it's mental growth when new information or skills are learned, and we transition from one level of understanding to another.

The natural world, created by God, reflects the elements of the spiritual world. As we look at the natural world, we see growth in plants—from seed to plant to the production of fruit. We see growth in animals from the newly born to maturity and fullness of life. We see the development of creativity and new thought—from idea to concept and development to final implementation.

Growth occurs in the natural world and in the believer's life as well. Psalm 1 says that the person who follows God, delights in His instruction, and implements it daily will be prosperous and productive. Production requires growth and change. This is supposed to happen. Transition is the process of change.

We are transformed—we grow and change—as we allow God's Spirit to reveal God's character and His truth in our lives.

> "But we all, with unveiled face, beholding as in a mirror the glory of the Lord, are being transformed into the same image from glory to glory, just as from the Lord, the Spirit."
> 2 Corinthians 3:18 NASB.

> "Therefore I urge you, brethren, by the mercies of God, to present your bodies a living and holy sacrifice, acceptable to God, which is your spiritual service of worship. And do not be conformed to this world, but be transformed by the renewing of your mind, so that you may prove what the will of God is, that which is good and acceptable and perfect."
> Romans 12:1-2 NASB

Your spirit is born-again, but your soul can and should be transformed—it should grow and change—by the revelation and application of God's Word. You hear His Word, you read it, you agree with it, you start to see life through its directives, and you apply it in your actions. The plan of God always contains the elements of growth and change.

When we learn how to grow, to transition, each day, then big changes won't be frightening when they need to occur. We'll face them just like we face every opportunity: with humor, excitement, hope, faith, belief in our abilities, and trust in God's strength and wisdom. He will see us through.

Waiting too long to transition.

You cannot accomplish anything of great worth without going outside of your comfort zone. Like Abraham, you have to leave the place of comfort to go into your promised land (Genesis 15:7). You cannot look back. You cannot go back. You cannot turn backward; that is sin; it's disobedience.

When you wait too long to transition to a new thing, you can block someone else from entering their next season, into the area that you currently serve or work. It's important to allow another person to transition into your current role or location. They are needed just as you were needed.

Holding on to the past—wanting to stay past the time of transition—denies God the opportunity to give you something bigger and better. An unwilling attitude to move forward means that God has no choice but to leave you behind. He cannot use you in the way that

He had planned if you are unwilling to move forward, unwilling to obey.

Why would you want to stay or go backward when *the new* is ahead of you? Why would you fear *the new* when God's perfect love for you obliterates and destroys fear? Fear of transition can be described as not trusting that God has good things for you in *the new*.

So, don't stay past the point where God inspires you to transition. Don't stay past the time of your season in a place. Move on when God tells you to move on.

Transitioning outside of God's will.

Here is a basic principle for life: Just because you see that something needs to be done or is wrong doesn't mean that you should do it or fix it.

When you try to do or fix something in your own wisdom and strength to meet a need or change a situation, you will deny God the opportunity to work in, with, and through you the way that He wants to work. You also may derail what God had really wanted you to do and deny the correct person the opportunity to handle that need or situation.

When Moses tried to fix a wrong with his own wisdom and strength he lost credibility, derailed his preparation, took a human life, and had to flee Egypt (Exodus 2:4-12). He chose to kill the Egyptian instead of another course of action. Pharaoh then tried to kill Moses (Exodus 2:15). Because of Moses' actions, the Israelites didn't respect him (Exodus 2:13-14).

Did God provide preparation, safety, and eventual direct communication with Moses? Yes. But we will never know what Moses' early course of life could have been.

The stages of transition.

There are stages in transition that lead to a shift into something or somewhere new.

Stage One—Knowledge

Knowledge that a transition will be occurring is usually accompanied by a sense of dissatisfaction. Dissatisfaction—the sense that something is going to change or something needs to change—is an indicator that you should pray. The dissatisfaction is necessary to get you to prepare for something new.

Stage Two—Preparation

In the case of both Moses and Jesus, the one who would provide freedom was in the world but had to mature. We see in Moses' life in Exodus 2:1-11 that time passed. Preparation occurred.

You can follow these steps to successfully walk through your time of preparation.

Step One – Plant seeds into your tomorrow.

Do the steps that God tells you to do. Get the details for the plan. Pray about them, and act on them as directed.

Step Two – Water the seeds by devouring God's Word.

In Psalm 1, the person who loves God's instruction is described as a tree planted by streams of water. They love God's instruction; therefore, they are planted by water. Plant yourself and prepare for explosive growth by immersing yourself in the water of God's Word, His instruction.

What happens when water in the form of rain or snow comes from the sky and makes contact with the earth? Water softens the ground and activates seeds that have been planted but have been dormant in the earth. You are activated for growth when you encounter God's Word. It will cause your *potential* to become *reality*. Isaiah 55:10-11 clearly states this principle.

> "For as the rain and the snow come down
> from heaven, and do not return there without
> watering the earth and making it bear and
> sprout, and furnishing seed to the sower and

bread to the eater; so will My word be which goes forth from My mouth; it will not return to Me empty, without accomplishing what I desire, and without succeeding in the matter for which I sent it." NASB

Begin to speak what God says about you in His Word.

Step Three – Allow God to bring your future to pass while you praise Him for it.

What does that look like? Praise from a New Testament perspective can be simply defined as *boasting about something that God has done.* We see examples of this in the New Testament when people were healed. The healed person praised God for the healing, telling others what God had done. That's praise.

Because we now know that Jesus has completed the work of redemption in which He provided healing, provision, and every good thing (Ephesians chapters 1 and 2), we can praise Him in faith. We believe that what we have asked for already belongs to us through the finished work of Jesus (Mark 11:23-24).

That would look something like this: "Father God, thank You that through Jesus' finished work on the cross and His resurrection, I now have the _____ that I have needed. Your Word says _____ , and I believe that. I receive what You have already provided, and I thank you for it. I praise You for the provision. You have already given it."

Step Four – Guard your mouth and don't speak against your past, present, or future.

What we say has incredible power. We know from natural experience that our words can have a positive or negative impact. Our words change the atmosphere in a room, they create or destroy relationships, they prepare for and preface action, and at times they are the catalyst for drastic change.

It's vital to ensure that what we are saying aligns with what God has shown us to do, agrees with what we have prayed and praised, and states God's view through His Word. Agree with God, His Word, and what you know to be true. Speak words that reflect your faith in God.

Stage Three—Positioning

Your preparation will help you to be positioned correctly. God wants to give you instruction that will position you in a sweet spot regardless of what is happening around you.

"The LORD directs the steps of the godly.
He delights in every detail of their lives."
Psalm 37:23 NLT

Seasons of a believer's life and ministry are not limited or defined by external circumstances. The will of the Lord does not change, and it is not dependent on what is happening in the world around you. You do something because God has directed you to do it, not because you're concerned for the future. You act out of faith not out of fear. This is faith that God has spoken to you and directed and inspired you. This is faith that He knows more than you do, and He not only sees the future but also all the intricacies of the present. Your faith in God is more than simple belief that He exists. It is a steadfast belief that He exists in your *now*. Hebrews 11:6 tells us to believe that He *is*. That's present tense. He *is* in your now. In every moment of your life, He *is*. Hebrews 11:6 also tells us that God's desire and consistent action is to reward people who diligently seek Him, who passionately pursue Him.

"And without faith it is impossible to please
Him, for He who comes to God must believe
that He is and that He is a rewarder of those
who seek Him." Hebrews 11:6 NASB

God wants to direct and position you so you are ready for the transition. You can ask Him to give you knowledge of the timing and process of release so you are ready.

Stage Four—Release

Release is when you leave the old season, the job, location, type of ministry, etc. This stage requires action on your part. Release is just as important as preparation. If you don't release on time, you can hinder your arrival into your *new*. You would then have a limited impact because you would not have released on time.

If you are listening to the Holy Spirit's direction, you will know when release should occur. There have been times when I have been praying about the correct time to leave, and I have had a prompting in my spirit with a specific amount of time. For example, in one case, I knew it would be at the end of a year. When that time came, I was ready to leave. I had prepared to leave well and to arrive well in my *new*. At other times, my husband and I had an alert that something would change in our location. The alert came many years prior to the actual release. As we got closer to the time of release, my spirit had a sense of expectation. That expectation alerted me to prepare. I asked God for details, and He directed me to sell some furniture and to begin final preparation by making repairs to our home. Then during prayer one day, I heard "Now" in my spirit. It was time to sell our house and look for a new one. It was the time of release. The house sold as a private sale in two hours. Within six weeks, we were living a new area in a new house that was sold to us almost fully furnished. I look back and can understand the preparation steps even better now. I see what God was doing even when we were simply in the knowledge stage. He is so good, and He always knows what we need. If we will obey Him, we will be ready for the final stage—arrival.

Stage Five—Arrival

This is the arrival into your *new*. Arriving well will include additional adjustments on your part. You're in the *new*, so the methods for work or life that you used in the past may not work well or be appropriate for the new opportunity. Ask God to show you what belongs in this season and what doesn't belong. You also may need to learn new skills. Embrace them as an opportunity to grow.

Arriving in the new season may seem strange, but the prompting and direction of the Holy Spirit is available. If you've been seeking God's direction and details as you've been walking through the other stages of transition, then the Holy Spirit will have the details that you need in this stage as well.

Change is a constant in the Christian life.

CHAPTER SEVEN

Disobedience is Dangerous

Impatience and fear pounded through King Saul. Where was Samuel? Seven days. He had waited seven days as Samuel had specified. The people were leaving, hiding, afraid of the advancing enemy army. He was the king; he had to *do* something. "Bring me the offerings," Saul shouted. "I'll do the sacrifice if Samuel can't be here on time."

As Samuel walked over the top of the gentle hill, he smelled the tang of smoke and saw its swirls dancing in the air. His eyes caught other movement and he recognized Saul who was walking toward him with his arms open and a smile on his face. But this was no time for joy.

"What have you done!" Samuel exclaimed.

"The people were leaving. You didn't come when you said you would. The enemy army was advancing. So I decided to make the offering," Saul said defiantly.

Samuel gritted his teeth and said, "You acted like a fool. You didn't obey God. You didn't do what He said to do. There will be repercussions because of your decision to do what you wanted to do. God has appointed someone else to be king because you refused to follow God's instruction. God wants someone who wants what He wants."

Saul reeled at Samuel's words, but he turned away and shouted for the army to get ready for war.

■ ■

Time had passed. Samuel was weary, but he took a deep breath and began to speak to the king and his army. Samuel sensed God's presence, and he knew that his words were not his own. "Saul, go and completely destroy the Amalekites, their king, and all that they own as a punishment for how they acted toward Israel while Israel was coming out of Egypt." Saul looked at Samuel and agreed.

Saul led the army away and into a fierce battle with the Amalekites. The sounds of war and the weight of death hung on the air as Israel's army triumphed.

"Let's raid their camp. You saw their armor, they must have supplies that rival that," shouted a soldier.

"Alright let's go!" yelled another.

With the rush of battle in their minds, Israel's army ransacked the Amalekites' encampment and took what they wanted. They ignored God's specific words through Samuel. They didn't completely destroy everything; they kept some things for themselves.

That night, God spoke to Samuel saying, "I regret that I have made Saul king, for he has turned back from following Me and has not carried out My commands."[1] Samuel grieved as he prayed through the night.

Samuel left home at first light, and with heavy footsteps he again traveled to confront Saul. When Saul saw Samuel, he confidently said, "I've done what God said to do. I've destroyed the Amalekites."

Samuel recoiled at Saul's words, and he asked, "Then why am I hearing the sounds of sheep and oxen?"

Saul began to defend himself, "Look, the people didn't completely follow your instructions because the Amalekites had some good things that could be sacrificed to God...."

Samuel cut him off. "Listen. Let me tell you what God said to me last night. God made you king, and He sent you on a mission, telling you to completely destroy the Amalekites. Why didn't you do what God said you should do?"

Saul persisted, "I did obey. I went on the mission. I did destroy the Amalekites, except their king. The people took some of the Amalekites' things so they could sacrifice them to God."

Samuel looked at Saul and began to speak on God's behalf. "Has the LORD as much delight in burnt offerings and sacrifices as in obeying the voice of the LORD? Behold, to obey is better than sacrifice, and to heed than the fat of rams. For rebellion is as the sin of divination, and insubordination is as iniquity and idolatry. Because you have rejected the word of the LORD, He has also rejected you from being king."[2]

There are some important points in God's words to Saul through Samuel.

First, God doesn't want what the world values. Our feeble attempts to give it to Him for His use if He specifically said that it didn't belong to us are blatant disobedience. Your good ideas are no substitute for knowing and following God's directions.

Second, God called Saul's attitude and action *rebellion, insubordination,* and *rejection* of the instruction.

We cannot lightly ignore what God tells us to do, thinking that there will be no corresponding results of our actions. Saul lost the kingdom because of his rebellion, insubordination, and rejection of what God had told him to do. Saul's attitude and actions disqualified him from continuing in the role of responsibility that God had placed in his life. God said that Saul's rebellion and insubordination was sin and idolatry.

*God will not tolerate you becoming
an idol in your life.*

God wants us to have a humble, submitted, obedient heart. He doesn't just want obedient actions; He wants complete obedience in our attitude as well. There is no place for personal arrogance when we follow God. Our will must be submitted to His.

There is no danger in submitting your will to God. He is not an abuser; He is the healer, the God of restoration. His directions are not oppressive (1 John 5:3); they are for our security and stability to provide the best environment for our growth.

With that in mind, let's take the first step toward changing our attitude and actions. It isn't difficult. We start with repentance, then we choose humility which leads to submission, and then we follow that with obedient actions. To fulfill your destiny, you must recognize the One who gave you that destiny and follow Him.

There are specific areas, attitudes, and actions that can divert us from God's will into disobedience. Identifying and determining to avoid them will help us to continue forward with God.

Selfishness

People often laugh about being in the will of God as if it's something flexible. It's not. God looks through eternity and positions people where they will have the greatest impact, the most benefit in the world. However, you can stop God's plan for your life. You can stop it and go a different direction, refusing to fulfill what He has called you uniquely to do. To truly fulfill the will of God you will need to not only use your faith in God, but you also will need to stop making decisions based solely on what *you* want to do. The attitude of, "It's my life and I choose to live it my way" has no place in a wholehearted commitment to God. That selfishness is arrogance and is the opposite of humility.

A life of faith is one of utter reliance on God and the direction of His Holy Spirit. Selfishness has no place in a life governed by faith. Selfishness denies God the opportunity to hold the primary place in our lives. The symptoms of selfishness are seen in churches around the world: people complain that the program they need is not available in their church; they live lives that are not holy and pure; they participate in gossip, tearing down people who are united to them through Jesus' shed blood; they sing songs about themselves and call it worship; and they focus on feelings and natural circumstances. All of those are symptoms of selfishness. They are indications that a person has not fully submitted to the lordship of Jesus Christ and they have not chosen to live a life that reflects the selfless love of God that has been "poured out within our hearts through the Holy Spirit who was given to us." Romans 5:5 NASB It is impossible to be spiritually mature, with something to offer the world, if you are focused only on what makes you comfortable or on what you want to do for yourself.

Selfishness will destroy every partnership and every opportunity for fellowship because it will demand its own way and will put the focus on what will bring about what is best for the selfish person.

The simplest display of selfishness can ruin your part of God's plan. "I want" are the two words that have the potential to destroy what God has created you to do. He doesn't even want you to say, "I want to do Your will." That implies something that you may want but you haven't yet begun to do. He wants you to say, "Yes, I am doing Your will now and forever." When you do what you are uniquely called and qualified to do, empowered by the Holy Spirit, you will not be able to be selfish.

Fulfilling God's will requires selfless love toward others.

"Love is patient and kind. Love is not jealous or
boastful or proud or rude. It does not demand
its own way. It is not irritable, and it keeps no
record of being wronged. It does not rejoice
about injustice but rejoices whenever the truth
wins out." 1 Corinthians 13:4-6 NLT

Fulfilling God's will requires reliance on God and
His strength. This is a complete denial of self, walking
away from doing things your way in your strength. We
don't see selfishness in the Acts 2:43-47 description of
the early Church. We see selflessness.

"Everyone around was in awe—all those
wonders and signs done through the apostles!
And all the believers lived in a wonderful
harmony, holding everything in common.
They sold whatever they owned and pooled
their resources so that each person's need
was met." MSG

Their selflessness was God's love in action being
displayed through His children. Selflessness is care
and compassion that motivates actions that benefit the
other person.

Distraction

When people are not at the right place at the right
time they miss the blessing of God for that season,

that time, and that location. They miss what God has planned for them. Distraction is a major cause of this.

A distraction is anything that takes your attention away from what God told you to do. A distraction is the opportunity to do something different. It may be a good initiative, an opportunity to help someone, a business opportunity, or a relationship.

The need or hunger for love can inspire you to continually look for someone to love or someone who will love you. When you are looking, you're not trusting God to show you His plan for the relationships in your life. Looking itself can be a distraction—something that takes your time and attention away from God or what He's given you to do.

A distraction also could be a business opportunity or a need that you are able to fill. If God did not tell you to do that, then participating in that opportunity or filling that need may be helpful to others, but it will take time away from what God told you to do. A distraction may be an opportunity with good intentions, but if it's not the opportunity for you, it will take you down the wrong path. It will steal your time—time meant for God's will for your life—and it may ultimately derail you.

*Someone's need should not dictate
your obedience to do what God told you to do.*

If God isn't directing you to do something, it is not the right thing for you. Even if it is something good or helpful, if God didn't tell you to focus on that or to do it, it's the wrong thing. Additionally, as long as you think something else is an *option*, you will be distracted from what you should be doing.

When a person's attention is distracted, they can only see through the distraction. Their reality is distorted by the wrong focus, and they will be diverted down the wrong path. The end result will be a divergence from what they were uniquely designed to do. That person's unique skills will be put aside, and they will begin to develop skills that are not specific to the season that they should be in. The result is: wrong place, wrong time, wrong people, wrong skills, limited victories, limited testimonies, increased struggle, which lead to derailment and destruction. The person begins to question everything, even their faith in God. Avoiding distraction is vital.

Following distraction is disobedience.

Be honest. You may have seen or even done things that you knew were not the right thing for you to do. You may even now be far off of the path where you started. It's not too late to change. Take this moment right now and ask God to forgive you. Submit your will to God's will and determine that you'll allow Him to direct your life by His Spirit. Then ask God to show you what to do to get back on the right path.

Obedience creates opportunity.
Disobedience denies the right opportunities from happening.

CHAPTER EIGHT

Obedience and Your Breakthrough Are Connected

Their feet were dragging through the tall grass, but the journey was almost over. They couldn't wait to be home. David heard the voices of his army mixed with the sound of their footsteps. Laughter. Then questioning.

"Do you see that smoke over the hill? That's close to our city."

"That's not close to the city, that *is* the city."

"What's wrong?"

"We need to move faster!"

"The city is burning. Move!"

They raced toward the smoldering remains of their houses and shops. Where were their wives and children? As they searched through the ruins, their anguish and anger was palpable.

"Where are they? Where's my family?

"Ah! My God! They're gone. They're all gone. They've been taken!"

"This is David's fault. He settled us here, and now I've lost everything."

"Kill him! Stone him. Stone David. It's his fault."

Shoving his way through the angry men, David found Abiathar, the priest. "Please bring me the ephod. I need to ask God whether we should pursue the marauders, and if so, will we catch them and recover our families."

God's answer was "Pursue, for you will surely overtake them, and you will surely rescue all."[1]

So David and his six hundred men pursued the Amalekites who had stolen everything, including families, and had burnt the city of Ziklag. David left two hundred exhausted men at Besore brook, and with the remaining four hundred men, he pushed forward until he reached the Amalekites' encampment.

David gathered the men together and said, "We're outnumbered, but we have God's promise that we'll defeat them and rescue our families. We're going to do this in God's strength. Trust Him."

They attacked the camp. The brutal battle raged for more than twenty hours until their final triumph when the enemy was destroyed with the exception of four hundred young men who escaped on camels. David and his four hundred men had rescued all of their families and retaken all of their stolen property.

"Let's go home," David said. "It's time. We're done, and God has kept us safe and restored everything."

We all want to see a victory, whether it's a change in our personal lives or in a challenge that we face. We all want a breakthrough to what is best.

I've been with Christians who confess that they will have a breakthrough in a certain area of life. They petition God for a breakthrough, and they eagerly anticipate a breakthrough. They sing and say that He's the God of the breakthrough. He is. His power is unlimited. But what do *we* need to do to *receive* a breakthrough?

We need to understand the following points.

There is no breakthrough without repentance.

Humility inspires obedience. Arrogance inspires disobedience. Arrogance has no place in a believer's life.

"Therefore *it* says, 'GOD IS OPPOSED TO THE PROUD, BUT GIVES GRACE TO THE HUMBLE.' Submit therefore to God. Resist the devil and he will flee from you. Draw near to God and He will draw near to you. Cleanse *your* hands, you sinners; and purify *your* hearts, you double-minded. Be miserable and mourn and weep; let your laughter be turned into mourning and your joy into gloom. Humble yourselves in the presence of the Lord, and He will exalt you." "Come now, you who say, 'Today or tomorrow we will go to such and such a city, and spend a year there and engage in business and make a profit.' Yet you do not know what your life will be like tomorrow. You are *just* a vapor that appears for a little while, and then vanishes away. Instead, *you ought* to say, 'If the Lord wills, we will live and also do this or that.' But as it is, you boast in your arrogance; all such boasting is evil. Therefore, to one who knows *the* right thing to do and does not do it, for him it is sin." James 4:6-10, 13-17 NASB

Many times, we choose to act like the description of arrogance and stubbornness seen in those scriptures. We say, "It's my life. I'm going to plan it the way I want to. I'm going to do *this* now. I'm going to do *that* tomorrow." If we have not asked God to direct us by His Spirit, we drastically increase our risk for failure, or we position ourselves to do the wrong thing that will take us out of God's plan.

It's time to repent from arrogance, pride, stubbornness, and an unwillingness to pursue the plan of God. Let's examine ourselves, and then repent.

There is no breakthrough without restoration.

Christians preach the need for revival, but we need something more than being revived or awakened. We need an internal spiritual revolution where carnality and stagnation are obliterated in God's presence. The word *revolution* is stronger than *revival*. We are being called to throw off one governing system for another— to throw off carnality and embrace a Spirit-directed life.

> "Therefore, brethren, since we have confidence to enter the holy place by the blood of Jesus, by a new and living way which He inaugurated for us through the veil, that is, His flesh, and since *we have* a great priest over the house of God, let us draw near to *God* with a sincere heart in full assurance of faith, having our hearts sprinkled *clean* from an evil conscience and our bodies washed with pure water."
> Hebrews 10:19-22 NASB

There must be a restoration of a living, active relationship and fellowship with God. We need a restoration of personal, authentic worship, and a commitment to time in His presence.

There is no breakthrough without obedience.

I'm speaking of obedience to God's plan for your life. This is submission to His will in every area of life with a focus of living a life that is worthy of Him. The following scriptures show what that looks like.

> "I therefore, a prisoner for the Lord, urge you to walk in a manner worthy of the calling to which you have been called, with all humility and gentleness, with patience, bearing with one another in love, eager to maintain the unity of the Spirit in the bond of peace." Ephesians 4:1-3 ESV

> "Therefore be imitators of God, as beloved children. And walk in love, as Christ loved us and gave himself up for us, a fragrant offering and sacrifice to God." Ephesians 5:1-2 ESV

> "But thanks be to God, who always leads us in triumph in Christ, and manifests through us the sweet aroma of the knowledge of Him in every place." 2 Corinthians 2:14 NASB

It's easy to say that the breakthrough is fully God's responsibility. Instead, let's do the hard thing and examine ourselves. Have we been putting the obligation on God and requiring Him to provide a breakthrough, when in fact we have been the ones who have restrained the breakthrough that He's already provided through Jesus Christ?

Whether you're facing a huge challenge, or you just want to see God's best happening in your life, stop and look at where you are in your relationship with Him. You can make any necessary shift and put yourself in the position to receive.

God cannot use a passive Christian.

CHAPTER NINE

Your First Step

We all have the opportunity to choose an active relationship with God. That relationship changes everything. It provides a sense of completion, of not being alone, and not needing to do everything with our limited intelligence and strength. That relationship can have real depth depending on our commitment to pursue depth.

When I hire an employee, I want to know who they are, their character and past history. Can I trust them? Can someone tell me how they will act in a given situation? Why would I not evaluate God's character. It's clearly found in the Bible. We can see how He acts, thinks, and speaks.

Based on a real, active, committed relationship with God through Jesus, you can take the first steps to a better, more meaningful life.

Obedience isn't a bad word. It's the result of knowing who God is and honoring Him.

Here are some thoughts about what obedience looks like within your relationship with God.

Give God first place in your life by recognizing His worth—who He really is. This means that you change your perspective about who should direct your life. Give Him the opportunity to demonstrate His wisdom by talking to Him and listening to what He says through the Bible and by His Spirit who is with you.

See yourself differently; you are *in Christ*. This means that you change the way that you respond to challenges. When you see beyond yourself and see things from God's view where you're seated in Christ, you'll stop complaining and start to speak what God says about you in the Bible.

Be willing to grow and change. Don't be afraid to trust God to help you to develop new skills. We hear a lot about emotional intelligence, but spiritual intelligence—an understanding of the depth of a Christian life—can positively affect your body, your mind, and your emotions. Spiritual things are eternal, and they are more important than natural things that decay.

Allow God to position you where you are uniquely qualified to fit. Accept His direction when He inspires you to help others with your skills and talents. Recognize that you are the only you that exists, and the person that you are has the capacity to help people in ways that no one else can. You are unique, and God wants to work with you to express the gifts He's given you.

And finally, follow Jesus' example in His relationship with the Father, in humility, and in selfless interactions with others. Represent Jesus in every area of your life. It's so much richer that way.

The process of adjusting to a life of obedience is: Decide. Do.

Notes

Chapter Two

1. 1 Samuel 8:7-9, *New American Standard Bible.*

Chapter Four

1. 1 Samuel 16:12, *New American Standard Bible.*

2. 1 Samuel 13:14, *New American Standard Bible.*

Chapter Seven

1. 1 Samuel 15:11, *English Standard Version.*

2. 1 Samuel 15:22-23, *New American Standard Bible.*

Chapter Eight

1. 1 Samuel 30:8, *New American Standard Bible.*

About the Author

Dr. Melody Lavin is the president and director of Victorious Living Ministries International™. Dr. Lavin establishes and directs Bible schools internationally, working with pastors and missions organizations to customize programs that will impact their nations.

Dr. Lavin is an author, a worship clinician, and an international speaker. She is a graduate of Rhema Bible Training College with a concentration in music ministry. She also has degrees in Theology and Biblical Studies, and a Ph.D. in Ministry.

Dr. Lavin is available to minister in your church or to your group with seminars and practical workshops, in church services, and for retreats. Her experience, diverse background, and humor provide a fresh perspective of life and ministry.

Email: melody@vlmi.org
Website: https://vlmi.org

www.ingramcontent.com/pod-product-compliance
Lightning Source LLC
Chambersburg PA
CBHW051546120626
46551CB00013B/1393

9798990656512